Advent Conversations

Lighting The Advent Wreath

Years A, B, and C

Richard J. Hull, II

Background Information
written by
Robert G. Alexander

CSS Publishing Company, Inc., Lima, Ohio

ADVENT CONVERSATIONS

For more information about CSS Publishing Company resources, visit our website at www.csspub.com.

ISBN 0-7880-1836-1

PRINTED IN U.S.A.

This resource is dedicated to
Riverside Avenue Christian Church
in Jacksonville, Florida,
whose members constantly strive
to understand God's truth
in today's issues and biblical texts.

Table Of Contents

Introduction

The dialogues in this resource were written as a way of bringing energy to the weekly lighting of the candles on the Advent Wreath. An attempt is made through these conversations to relate the lectionary reading from the prophets to a contemporary concern. It is hoped that with well-rehearsed and presented conversations worshipers will feel like participants in the candle lighting rather than observers.

The dialogues were written over a period of three years. Some of them may seem dated to particular events that were taking place at that time. Those who use these dialogues should edit and adapt them to their situations and concerns.

Several of the dialogues were written with particular members of a congregation in mind as presenters. Personal references in the conversations may have to be adapted to the particular presenters in another setting. Please feel free to do so.

Most importantly, use these dialogues to inspire the preparation of your own Advent Wreath conversations.

Advent Wreath Lighters' Instructions

Thank you for agreeing to deliver a dialogue and light the candles on the Advent Wreath.

Each dialogue is based on an Old Testament scripture. The words of the prophets have often been used to point the way toward understanding who Jesus is. Please read the designated scripture so you can understand the dialogue better. The dialogue relates the theme of the scripture to a contemporary concern.

1. Please memorize the dialogue. If it is a memorized conversation, it will have a better flow and thus a better impact on the listeners.

2. Come forward without introduction at the designated time in the bulletin.

3. Present the dialogue from the chancel steps.

4. Remember these three rules about speaking in public:
   a. Speak more loudly than you think you need to.
   b. Speak more slowly than you think you need to.
   c. Put pauses between phrases and sentences and some words.

5. Please practice your presentation several times.

Year A

First Sunday Of Advent
A Dialogue for New Residents
Based on Isaiah 2:1-5

1· Well, we haven't lived in this town very long but it's starting to feel like home.

2: I know what you mean. At that conference I went to last week I saw my friend Tom.

1: Tom, your high school friend from back home?

2: That's him. When I told him where we lived now, he asked, "Where is that?" He knew what state but didn't know where in the state. I thought to myself, "You dummy, this is an important city. You should know where it is."

1: That is exactly what I mean. I find myself taking pride in our new home and wanting to brag about it and wanting the rest of the country to know what a great place we live in.

2: There are so many good things going on here.

1: Perhaps hometown pride was what the prophet Isaiah was feeling and more so when he talked about Jerusalem and its temple as the Mountain of The Lord.

2: I know that passage:
"Come, let us go up to the mountain of the Lord,
that he may teach us his ways
and that we may walk in his paths.
For out of Zion shall go forth instruction,
and the word of the Lord from Jerusalem."

9

1: And then follows the great line:
"They shall beat their swords into plowshares,
and their spears into pruning hooks,
nation shall not lift up sword against nation,
neither shall they learn war any more."

2: So, I think the prophet took great pride in the city of Jerusalem and proclaimed that God's peace could come from it to the whole world.

1: I suppose all people take pride and want good things to come from their city.

2: And if we would be like Isaiah and focus pride in God instead of ourselves, then perhaps nations would get along.

1: Let's light an Advent candle to encourage us to walk in the light of the Lord here in our new hometown.

Light the first candle.

Year A

Second Sunday Of Advent
A Dialogue for Two Friends
Based on Isaiah 11:1-11

1: Well, we decorated the Christmas tree at our house last night.

2: That's always fun. Anything special about the way you do it?

1: Yeah, now that you mention it. We have some old bows, pre-manufactured bows, that we put on the tree every year. We got them the first year we were married. I was still in school and we were going back home for Christmas, but we wanted to have some kind of tree in our apartment for our first Christmas.

2: It was important to start family traditions.

1: So we bought a little artificial tree that came complete with decorations for $6.00. Those bows we put on last night were part of that set. We've put them on for 25 years now.

2: And it brings back memories?

1: Lots of them — remembering when we were first married, and how much we loved each other. And even more than memories, it causes us to stop and think about our life now and how we can continue making good memories.

2: Kind of like the shoot of Jesse.

1: The what?

2: The shoot of Jesse; Jesse was the Father of Israel's greatest king, David. Almost since the end of David's reign the people of

11

Israel had imagined a new king, a Messiah who would be like David and return the people to greatness.

1: So the shoot of Jesse was a poetic way of referring to someone who would be like the Messiah. Someone who would be a great leader and create peace and prosperity.

2: That's right, Isaiah said it this way:
"A shoot shall come out of Jesse.
The Spirit of the Lord shall rest on him.
With righteousness he shall judge the poor.
The wolf shall live with the lamb.
They will not hurt or destroy on all my holy mountain."

1: So you are saying that the bows we put on the Christmas tree are like the shoot of Jesse. They help us remember the past in a way that makes the present and the future better.

2: Well said. And Advent candles remind us that we are waiting for the real joy of Christmas. Let's light one.

Light the first and second candles.

Third Sunday Of Advent
A Dialogue for Two Friends
Based on Isaiah 35:1-10

1: Have you been Christmas shopping yet?

2: I sure have. I fought the mall traffic yesterday. It about cost me my religion.

1: Traffic was bad, huh?

2: Bad is right. I don't know why with all the road taxes we pay they can't build more roads to get us there.

1: I have a theory about roads. The more we build the worse the traffic gets. Once it becomes easier to get someplace, the more people will drive to get there; so the need for more roads increases.

2: You think we should have fewer roads?

1: I think if we tore down some highways, then it would be too much hassle for people to drive across town to the superstore, and there would be more neighborhood stores and more people would shop closer to home.

2: You're probably right. I drove ten miles the other day to save ten cents on soap. I just had to jump on the highway, and I was there in ten minutes. But traffic was slow coming back. I spent more on gas than I saved.

1: The prophet Isaiah knew something about road construction. He talked about a highway called the "Holy Way." He said:
"It shall be for God's people.
No traveler, not even fools, shall go astray."

2: Sounds good to me. I get lost just backing out of my driveway.

1: Isaiah imagined a highway without dangers. He said:
   "No lion shall be there,
   nor shall any ravenous beast come up on it;
   they shall not be found there,
   but the redeemed shall walk there."

2: Imagine that, a highway without dangers. God, the ultimate air bag.

1: You got it. Isaiah's road is one that leads to God. God will help us through the hassles and traffic jams and dangers of life.

2: Let's light a candle to illumine the way on God's highway.

Light the first, second, and third candles.

Fourth Sunday Of Advent
A Dialogue for Two High School Students
Based on Isaiah 7:10-16

1: Have you heard whose baby is going to be Jesus in this year's Christmas pageant?

2: No, have you?

1: No, but I am sure if they pick the Williams' baby, the Strongs are going to be mad.

2: Isn't that just like people? We turn a joyous occasion into a cause for jealousy and fighting. Life is so messed up.

1: Whoa, you're on a roll. What's got you going?

2: You know what I mean. Look around, read the paper, watch the news.

1: I do.

2: Don't you pay attention? Domestic violence, gang warfare, genocide, hunger, starvation, poverty — trouble is everywhere. Not to mention the constant threat that some terrorist will get a nuclear bomb and destroy a whole country.

1: I know it can be bad.

2: It is bad. I don't know why the Williamses and the Strongs ever had a baby. I wouldn't want to bring a baby into this world.

1: You wouldn't?

2: No way! Would you?

1: Well, I'm glad my parents had me! And yours you. If you hadn't been born, I'd be short one friend.

2: Yeah, but life wasn't so bad when we were born.

1: It wasn't? Have you been asleep in history class? You've never heard about the Cold War or World War II or the Depression or the Bubonic Plague?

2: Yes, of course I have.

1: And you must have been asleep in Sunday school too. Don't you remember what Isaiah the prophet said to King Ahaz?

2: No, what?

1: Well, Isaiah's country was being attacked by countries on both sides. It looked bleak, and Isaiah said, "A young woman is with child and shall bear a son, and shall name him Immanuel." That means God with us.

2: I know that. I do know something, but I thought it was said about Jesus.

1: Matthew quoted Isaiah when describing Jesus' coming birth. When Jesus was born, times weren't very good either. Israel was ruled by Rome, Herod was a corrupt ruler, and that's the very time when God decided to become a baby.

2: I hear you. Even in tough times, life goes on. It's like that poster on your bedroom wall that reads, "Every time a baby is born, it is God's way of saying life should continue."

1: Merry Christmas! Bingo! You got it! Let's light the Advent candles instead of cursing the darkness.

Light the four candles.

Years A, B, C
Christmas Eve — Christ Candle
A Conversation for A Family
Based on Isaiah 9:2-7

(Assign parts according to number of family members.)

1: I'm glad our family can be together in [name of your town] to celebrate Christmas. Do you realize that in the southern hemisphere, like in Argentina, that it is now summer, and the days are the longest of the year?

2: That's why I think in the northern hemisphere we find this passage especially meaningful at Christmas:
"The people who walked in darkness
have seen a great light,
on them light has shined."

3: But there are some nations where parts of the scripture would really speak better than they do to us. Imagine if we lived in a country ruled by a dictator or in a nation at war.

4: Good point. In those counties these verses would really give hope:
"You have multiplied the nation,
you have increased its joy.
For the yoke of their burden,
and the bar across their shoulders,
the rod of the oppressor, you have broken."

5: And this one too:
"For all the boots of the tramping warriors
and all the garments rolled in blood
shall be burned as fuel for the fire."

6: But there are some passages in which Isaiah speaks to everyone, everywhere, with the same power:
    "For unto us a child is born, unto us a son is given,
    and the government shall be upon his shoulders
    and his name shall be called Wonderful, Counselor,
    Mighty God, Everlasting Father, Prince of Peace."

7: Let's light the Christ candle to remember that unto us a Son is born.

Light the four candles, and, finally, the Christ candle.

Year B

First Sunday Of Advent
A Dialogue for Father and Son
Based on Isaiah 64:1-9

S: Dad, don't you ever wish that God would really become obvious? You know, like as obvious as an earthquake or as clear as when a fire burns a forest or when heat boils water.

D: Why do you ask?

S: Well, you know. I'd like the people who don't love God to see what God is really like and be afraid of God's power.

D: Maybe you're thinking of some of the stories in the Bible when it seemed like God led the Israelites against the other nations.

S: That's right. Like when Pharaoh let the people go. Like when the Israelites took over the Promised Land. I don't think we see God doing those kinds of things any more.

D: Yeah, I know what you're saying. But I still think those who wait patiently for God, and who live their lives rightly, and who remember the ways of God know how great God is.

S: But sometimes it seems like God is hiding from us.

D: Yes, I know. I don't doubt that God has times of getting angry with our sins. And in our sin, we are embarrassed to be in God's presence, and it seems like God is far away.

S: Yeah, we're like that dirty cloth on the floor in the garage. No one wants to pick it up and clean it; so it just gets more dirty and more useless.

D: Do you think it has to be that way?

S: No, of course not. God's the creator and can make of us what God wants. We're like clay on a potter's wheel. If there is a flaw in us, God can remake us.

D: Why don't we light a candle to remind us, from now until Christmas, that when it seems God is angry with us, it won't always be that way.

S: Good idea.

Light the first candle.

Year B

Second Sunday Of Advent
A Dialogue for Two Older Adults
Based on Isaiah 40:1-11

1. You know we've seen a lot of war in our life time.

2: That's the truth. World War II,

1: The Korean Conflict,

2: Vietnam,

1: The Gulf War,

2: And the Cold War.

1: You know, it's kind of nice this year that we aren't actually at war. Makes Christmas seem more like Christmas.

2: Yeah. It's kind of like the time when Isaiah said, "Comfort, comfort my people. Speak tenderly to Jerusalem that her warfare is ended."

1: Still, I heard someone say one time, "Peace is more than the absence of war." I think we need to remember that.

2: That's for sure. The seeds for war are always being planted whenever injustice continues. So we need to keep working for peace. Isaiah said it this way:
"Prepare the way of the Lord,
make straight in the desert
a pathway for our God."

1: I don't know that our generation always did the best we could, but everything is going to belong to a new generation someday soon. Our days are about over. Do you know what I fear we failed at most?

2: What's that?

1: I'm afraid we failed to help the younger generations know God the way we were taught to know God.

2: You may be right. There was no question when we were young but that "the word of God would stand forever."

1: Isaiah again?

2: That's right, and here's something else Isaiah said:
    "God will feed his flock like a shepherd;
    he will gather the lambs in his arms."

1: Let's light a candle to remind us that the way to true peace is with God.

2: Like Isaiah would say, "A herald of good tidings."

Light the first and second candles.

Year B
Third Sunday Of Advent
A Dialogue for Two Friends
Based on Isaiah 61:1-4, 8-10

1: (*Stands and flips a coin*)

2: Is there a football game starting around here?

1: No, I'm just trying to decide something.

2: What?

1: I'm trying to decide if God is winning or losing.

2: Winning or losing what?

1: Winning or losing whatever game God is playing.

2: Tell me more.

1: "The spirit of the Lord," says Isaiah, anoints us "to bring good news to the oppressed, to bind up the brokenhearted, to proclaim liberty to the captives, and to release prisoners." So is God winning or losing? As I see it: the Tutsies are killing the refugees in Zaire; child labor laws are being violated all over the world; even in this country, drug use is going up, and we can't build jails fast enough. So maybe God's losing.

2: Maybe, but Nicaragua just had its second democratic election, we just elected a president, world starvation is down except in places of political unrest, violent crime is less than it has been, even marriage seems to be fairing better. So maybe God's winning.

1: That's why I am flipping this coin.

2: Fair enough. But what about you?

1: What about me?

2: Is God winning or losing with you?

1: What's that got to do with anything?

2: Well, Isaiah also said, "My whole being will exult in my God for he has clothed me with garments of salvation." So how's your wardrobe?

1: I bought a whole new outfit for Christmas.

2: Can you wear it on your heart?

1: (*Ponders a moment then with confidence*) Yes, I can. I can wear God's clothes: the garment of salvation and the robe of righteousness.

2: Good. How about lighting a candle to celebrate with joy that at least God is winning in your life.

Light the first, second, and third candles.

Fourth Sunday Of Advent
A Dialogue for Two Teenagers
Based on Isaiah 11:1-10

1: Hey, I need a friend.

2: Hey, don't we all.

1: Of course, but I need one right now. That Bible passage we read in Sunday school got me thinking.

2: (*Sniffs*) Yeah, I can smell you burning up your brain. Just kidding. What's the problem?

1: Well, there was that stuff about the stump of Jesse.

2: That's right. Jesse was King David's father. And the passage said something good would come from that family. Teacher thought it referred to Jesus.

1: Yeah, whatever. Anyway this stump was going to produce a spirit of wisdom and understanding.

2: I remember.

1: And this stump was going to make it possible for a wolf and a lamb to live together.

2: Sounds impossible to me. But what's it got to do with you? You don't even like animals.

1: Not animals I'm thinking of, but Terry.

2: Terry, your best friend since second grade? Terry, your bosom buddy all these years?

1: Yeah, until last semester when she told the teacher I was having trouble in Algebra. She asked me to stay after class. I was totally embarrassed.

2: I know you haven't spoken to Terry since. That's how you and I got to be friends.

1: Yeah, but it's Christmas, and Terry and I have always gotten each other some special surprise gift for Christmas. Would it hurt anything if I went ahead and got a surprise gift this year?

2: Sounds like a good way even to give God some glory. But one thing. Can we still be friends, too?

1: Sure we can. I'll even let you light the Advent wreath candle for me.

Light the four candles.

Year C

First Sunday Of Advent
A Dialogue for A Married Couple
Based on Jeremiah 33:14-16

W: I have made so many promises about Christmas, and it's not even December.

H: I know what you mean. My dad made me promise we would have Christmas dinner with them this year.

W: Uh-oh, I promised my parents.

H: Uh-oh, is right.

W: The kids wanted me to promise to get them the latest Sega Genesis game.

H: And they made me promise not to tell you what they are getting you for Christmas.

W: Lots of promises. Still, making promises seems to be a good Christmas tradition, don't you think?

H: In what way?

W: Well, promises and God seem to go together. When we got married, we promised before God to love, honor, and cherish each other as long as we lived. We haven't always succeeded, but still it seems like a good promise to make.

H: That's right, and when the kids were born, we promised, right here during worship, in the presence of God, to provide for their emotional, physical, and spiritual needs.

W: Maybe that's why the prophet Jeremiah is often read at Advent. Jeremiah wrote: "Thus says the Lord, 'The days are coming when I will fulfill the promise I made to my people. I will cause a righteous Branch to spring up for David and he will execute justice and righteousness in the land.' "

H: I think that's the same passage where God promises: "The people will be saved and live in safety."

W: You're right. Let's light a candle to remind us of the promises of God.

H: We'll light it every week while we prepare the way of the Lord, and it can remind us of the promises of God.

Light the first candle.

Year C

Second Sunday Of Advent
A Dialogue for Two Friends
Based on Malachi 3:1-4

1. I know it's still early to ask, but are you ready for Christmas?

2: Gift buying, yes. I did that early. Now I am starting to get ready for Christmas dinner. All the children and grandchildren will be home, and we are including a new couple from church in our plans. I like a big Christmas dinner.

1: I know what you mean. When I was growing up, we had three tables full of aunts and uncles and cousins every year. The last few years, it's been just George and me and my sister. But this year both kids will be home.

2: That's good. Do you know what I like best? I like polishing the silver and bleaching and starching the tablecloth.

1: Really. Silver takes so much work, and these days I'm only using it every few years.

2: I know, but it feels so good when the tarnish gives way to a bright shine and when the tablecloth gleams and sits stiffly on the table. It just cheers me up.

1: That reminds me of our Bible study this week. Malachi said: "The day of the Lord is coming like a silver refiner's fire and like fullers' soap, and the people will be refined like silver and present righteous offerings to the Lord."

2: Yeah, that makes sense. I'm not trying to show off by using shiny silver and bleached tablecloths. I use them to remind me always to show my best to God.

29

1: Let's light one of these candles to remind us this Christmas that not only our silver but our whole lives should shine before God.

2: Good idea. I have already prepared gifts, I'm preparing the silver, but most of all I need to get myself ready for Jesus to come.

Light the first and second candles.

Year C

Third Sunday Of Advent
A Dialogue for Two Youth
Based on Zephaniah 3:14-20

1: *(Sings)* "Well, there's no place like home for the holidays ..."

2: What a corny old Christmas song.

1: Yeah, I guess, but I like it.

2: Did you ever notice that every generation has its own kind of music?

1: Yeah, like our grandparents listened to crooners like Frank Sinatra.

2: And our parents say they invented rock 'n' roll.

1: And the rap music of our generation drives them crazy.

2: So, what's that got to do with that corny old Christmas song?

1: Well, I noticed that Christmas music stays the same, generation after generation. People still sing the same songs.

2: You're right. Maybe Christmas music is the fulfillment of what Zephaniah said.

1: Zephaniah. Speaking of corny, that's a corny name.

2: If you had been in Sunday school, you would have known that Zephaniah was a prophet. He said:
"Sing aloud, O Jerusalem.
The Lord is in your midst.

31

I will save the lame and the outcast.
I will bring you home."

1: You're right. Old Zephaniah would have liked Christmas songs. The spirit of Christmas is a spirit of singing, of feeling God's presence, of doing good for others, a time for being at home.

2: Let's light a candle to keep us in the spirit of Christmas until we celebrate Christ's birth.

Light the first, second, and third candles.

Fourth Sunday Of Advent
A Dialogue for Two Fathers
Based on Micah 5:2-5a

1: Were you with your wife when your kids were born?

2: Yeah, both of them. Why?

1: Well, I remember that experience every year just before Christmas. I was scared to death, and there were two doctors and three nurses in the room.

2: I remember. I was afraid I was going to faint.

1: So, how must Joseph have felt? Alone with Mary far from home, no family, and she goes into labor in a cow stall.

2: I would have fainted dead away.

1: Still, I wouldn't have missed it for the world. One of the most amazing and precious moments of my life.

2: So, imagine if your kid had been the son of God, how special that time would be.

1: I'll bet Micah was present when his kids were born.

2: Micah who?

1: Micah, the prophet. He described the coming time of God as a birth experience. He said:
"God shall give them up
until the time when she who is in labor
has given birth.

Then he will stand and feed his flock
in the strength of the Lord."

2: Let's light these candles to remind us of the strength of the Lord
that comes to us in the birth of Jesus.

Light the four candles.

The Advent Wreath

The Advent wreath is believed to be of Lutheran origin, although the use of evergreens and leafy crowns dates well into the deep time of the pagan, Graeco-Roman world. An evergreen, closed circle wreath, the Advent wreath has four white candles symbolizing God's Son as the light of the world in the darkness of both time and season, the winter solstice. Sometimes a taller, white candle, known as the Christ candle, is placed in the wreath's center. The use of a closed circle of evergreen boughs portrays the creation, as, even when in the deep sleep of winter, life continues without end.

Typically, in sanctuary use, the Advent wreath is placed on a stand in or near the chancel. The home wreath usually is placed flat on a table suitable for a home worship center, with the candles upright. Originally, the Advent wreath practice probably started in the home and, over time, only gradually found its way into the church sanctuary, possibly due to the early church's concern over past pagan usages of evergreens as well as the need for a period of preparation before Christmas. Nevertheless, home wreath practices have continued and are a source of enrichment for home Advent devotions.

Candles may vary in color according to congregation and family custom. For example, the four candles might be the liturgical, seasonal color of violet or perhaps purple, emphasizing Remembrance, Royalty (Kingship), or both. In any event, Jesus as Light of the World, overcoming the darkness of the world and of the season, is the dominant theme. Sometimes bits of purple ribbon are tied to the four candles. Occasionally, the third candle is rose or pink. Others have it four red candles plus one center white candle. In any event, there is rich symbolism inherent in these color choices. It should be noted that there is no liturgically required color for these candles, other than flowing from custom and good sense of the season.

Beginning four Sundays before Christmas, one candle is lighted each week, penetrating the dark world to which Jesus, as

The Coming One of prophecy, would burst forth, in the fullness of time. Although, historically, the Advent wreath may be traced to pagan sources, the Christian church absorbed, redefined, and sacralized not only the season of its use but its meaning, no less than light given to the darkness of a heathen world. For example, "some believe the idea of the wreath originated in Scandinavia where during the shortest days of the year, men lighted candles on a wheel and prayed to the god of light that he would turn the wheel of the earth's orbit to the sun again and lengthen the days" (Victorson, p. 7). We should have no concern about this converting of ancient customs in that these very same peoples were converted to Christianity in part through transformed and sacralized customs. In this sense the Advent wreath becomes gift both of and for the Christ Child.

Advent then, with its rich and robust symbol of the wreath, begins the Christian ecclesiastical calendar the first Sunday nearest November 30 (or some prefer to state it as the first Sunday after November 24) in the great Christmas cycle, with two *comings*: the first, that of the Christ Child at Christmas; and the second, that of Christ, the promise of the return, the Parousia, the second coming of Christ. The first *coming* is that of the fulfillment of prophecy, of God *doing a new thing*, seen as God entering the world, bringing the good news of salvation and the light, showing the way out of darkness; and the second *coming*, the promise of the return, that of Christ *coming* to judge the world. This *promise* dimension, this eschatological reserve, is clearly set forth in the earliest, extant, written description of the Eucharist in scripture, that of the Apostle Paul in 1 Corinthians 11:23 and specifically that of verse 26: "For as often as you eat this bread and drink the cup, you proclaim the Lord's death *until he comes*."

The use of candles and the light provided was an important part of Graeco-Roman midwinter festivities. Wax tapers were given as gifts during the Roman festival of Saturnalia. To early Christians, the lights and bonfires of this event took on the added significance of "Jesus as the Light of the World."

In many parts of the world today, Advent candles *reflect the dawning season and remind us of the coming of the Light*. The

36

pagan Romans, however, believed in a god of seed-time, Saturn, and the festivities of Saturnalia were by all accounts boisterous. The halls and homes were "decked with boughs of laurel and of green trees, with lighted candles and with lamps — the hovering spirits of darkness were afraid of light" (Count et al, pp. 34, 37). Of course, the Romans thought all of this was grand fun, but to the Christians, the god of Saturnalia and its festivities were abominations. At first, the emerging church forbade any recognition or participation but, after much struggle, "finally succeeded in taking the merriment, the greenery, the lights, and gifts from Saturn and giving them to the Babe of Bethlehem."

The idea of crowns and wreaths was well-known to both pagans and Christians. The *Civic Crown* was one of the most revered honors among ancient Romans. It was given for saving the life of a citizen in battle. A *wreath* of oak leaves and acorns worn at important events, it marked a person to be greatly honored. Sometimes laurel wreaths were civic crowns awarded to champion athletes. And the symbolism of the rose signified matters to be held in confidence (*sub rosa*, for "under the rose").

In Christianity, when a rose candle is used either for the third candle or the Christ candle, it can easily resonate with Mary's treasuring "all these things in her heart." On many occasions even Jesus cautioned his disciples *not* to speak of *these things*. The rose is also a symbol for the *Kingdom* of God and the Christ(mas) rose, interestingly enough, is a white flower (not unlike the familiar iris), known as black hellebore, from the color of its roots. *Flora's Feast*, an 1890 painting by Walter Crane, is perhaps familiar to many who are interested in the lore of Advent and the Christmas Cycle. For instance, it has been suggested in a symbolically sound manner, that the color black is the true color of Advent in that the world was given to darkness in content and season and the lighting of such grimly colored candles shows starkly the light which is coming into the world.

The early Christian fellowship was mainly a nighttime worship event and much of Jesus' nights were spent in prayer. And who can forget the Light of the World being arrested at night by the *light* of torches and the treachery of betrayal? Persecutions equaled meetings at night and secret signs, such as that of the fish.

Sub rosa, so shine the candles of the Coming One and the One To Come. The early fellowship was also enriched by the backdrop and the teaching of the kindling of the Shabbat candles. Our Advent wreath and candles herald the coming of the Messianic Age in the fullness of time and as was foretold.

The Christian Calendar begins with the Advent crown wreath of evergreen and candles, overcoming the darkness of time and spirit, and ends with a civic crown wreath of mockery, ridicule, and scorn, a crown of thorns — and the final victory of the Cross! Darkness has been overcome and salvation is at hand!

Robert G. Alexander

The following is a list of the principal authorities consulted in the writing of this essay. The writer acknowledges his debt with gratitude.

Treatises

Christmas, Customs and Traditions, their History and Significance, Clement A. Miles, Dover Publications, Inc., New York, New York, 1912, 1976.

The Christmas Almanac, Gerald & Patricia Del Re, Doubleday & Company, Inc., Garden City, New York, 1979.

4000 Years of Christmas, A Gift from the Ages, Earl W. Count, Ph.D., Alice Lawson Count, Ulysses Press, Berkeley, California, 1997.

Liturgy and Literature, Selected Essays, James Allen Cabaniss, University of Alabama Press, 1970.

Microsoft® Encarta® 98 Encyclopedia, Microsoft Corporation, "Civic Crown," "Crown," "Flower Symbolism."

The New Oxford Annotated Bible, New Revised Standard Version, Oxford University Press, 1991, 1994, New York, New York, 1989.

A Book of Christmas, William A. Sansom, McGraw-Hill Book Company, New York, New York, 1968.

Floral Art In the Church, Jack Inman, Abingdon Press, Nashville, New York, 1968.

Programs For Advent and Christmas, Vincie Alessi, Ed. (Marsha West), Judson Press, Valley Forge, Pennsylvania, 1978, 1980.

Handbook of Christmas Programs, William Hendricks & Cora Vogel, Baker Book House Company, Grand Rapids, Michigan, 1978.

Worship Resources For the Christian Year, Charles L. Wallis, Ed., Harper & Brothers, New York, New York, 1954.

Christmas Wreaths, Steve Sherman, The Stephen Greene Press, Inc., Lexington, Massachusetts, 1987.

Doxology — The Praise of God in Worship, Doctrine, and Life, Geoffrey Wainwright, Oxford University Press, New York, New York, 1980.

Pamphlets
"The Story of the Advent Wreath," Reverend Frans A. Victorson, Fortress Press, 5008 1 73.

"Living Advent, a daily companion to the Lectionary," Cycle C, Julia Dugger, Liguori Publications, 1994.

Jewish Calendar, Chabad-Lubavitch, 1998/1999.